# Gold






*Written by Paul Shipton*
*Illustrated by Red Giraffe*

## Gold is a beautiful metal

In the Olympic Games, the winners receive gold medals. The World Cup football trophy is gold. At the Oscars in Hollywood, the actors receive gold statues. Why is this? Many people love this expensive yellow metal and like to wear gold jewellery. Gold does not change in water or air. It always shines.

Gold is a soft metal. Jewellery makers add other metals to make gold stronger.

## Uses of gold

Gold is a very useful metal. It is easy to make into new shapes. It can be very thin and very long. One gram of gold can make a wire more than three kilometres long!

Electricity travels well through gold. This means it is useful in electronics. There are very small pieces of gold inside some computers and mobile phones. There is gold on satellites in space and even on astronauts' helmets!

A satellite in space

## Finding gold

Gold is not easy to find. People usually dig mines under the ground to find it. There are many gold mines in South Africa. Some of these mines are very deep, sometimes 4,500 metres under the ground.

Gold mining is difficult, dangerous work.

There is very little gold in the world. This is why gold is expensive. There is gold in the sea, but it is very hard to reach. The biggest piece of gold in the world came from Australia. It weighed more than 71 kilograms.

**The Welcome Stranger Nugget**

# The history of gold

## The Egyptians

Howard Carter working in Egypt

People first used gold thousands of years ago. We know that the ancient Egyptians loved gold.

In 1922, an archaeologist called Howard Carter discovered the tomb of the Egyptian pharaoh*, Tutankhamun. When he opened the stone door, Carter was very surprised. There was gold everywhere.

* A pharaoh was an ancient Egyptian king.

The body of the pharaoh was inside a gold coffin. It was 3,000 years old. You can see Tutankhamun's gold mask in a museum.

*The mask weighs more than ten kilograms.*

## The Greeks

In ancient Greece, they used gold to make coins and jewellery. Greek myths show how important gold was to them.

- There was a special tree with three gold apples. Only gods could pick these apples.
- Helios, the god of the sun, had a chariot of gold.
- Everything turned to gold when King Midas touched it. Soon Midas was not happy. His food turned to gold, his drink turned to gold … even his daughter turned to gold!

*Helios, the god of the sun, and his chariot of gold.*

## The Romans

The Romans also used gold for money. They collected gold from many different countries around the world.

***This gold coin shows the head of the Roman Emperor Augustus.***

***Gold in the ground***

In 2000, an archaeologist discovered forty-three gold Roman coins in London. Maybe they belonged to a Roman soldier?

# The Incas and the Aztecs

Both the Incas in South America and the Aztecs in Central America used gold to make beautiful objects.

***The Aztecs were in Mexico. The Incan empire covered parts of Chile, Peru and Ecuador.***

The sun was very important to the Incas. They called gold 'the sweat of the sun'. They made many gold objects for their temples and shrines.

In the 16th century, Spanish explorers travelled to South and Central America. They conquered the Aztecs and the Incas. They took many beautiful gold figures back to Europe. People melted lots of these figures to use the gold again.

***In 1532, Francisco Pizarro conquered the Incas with only 200 soldiers.***

### *The City of Gold*

The first European explorers were very interested in stories about the city of *El Dorado*. Many explorers looked for this city, but they never found it.

## Pirates

Not all of the gold from South and Central America reached Europe. Some ships sank in storms. In 1715, a Spanish ship sank near the Florida coast. In the 1960s an archaeologist discovered some of the ship's gold.

Sometimes pirates attacked the ships and stole the gold. There was a very famous pirate called Blackbeard. People say that he stole and buried lots of gold somewhere along the coast of the USA.

***Blackbeard's real name was Edward Teach. Did he really bury lots of gold? Nobody knows.***

## Gold Rush

In 1848, somebody discovered gold in California, in the USA. Thousands of people from all around the world rushed there to find gold. Some people looked for gold in mines. Others looked for small pieces of gold in rivers. Some people became very rich, but most people found nothing.

***This person is looking for little pieces of gold at the bottom of a river. He separates the gold from mud and small rocks.***

***Fool's Gold***

Some people found shiny yellow rocks like this. It is not real gold. It is sometimes called 'Fool's Gold'.

## Fort Knox

Some governments still have lots of gold. The government of the USA has more gold bars than any other country. It keeps more than 8,000 tonnes of gold at a place called Fort Knox.

The gold at Fort Knox is very safe. In the James Bond film *Goldfinger*, criminals try to steal the gold from Fort Knox. Of course, James Bond stops them!

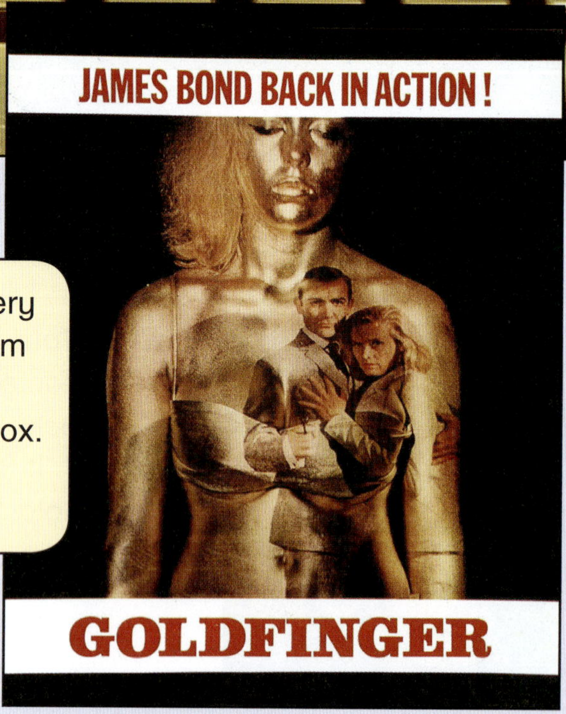

# Pirate's Gold

*Written by Paul Shipton*
*Illustrated by Red Giraffe*

My name is Megan and this is my family's incredible story.

One day my dad decided to open a Pirate Museum. He loved the history of pirates. So we moved into an old house by the sea. A long time ago the house belonged to a famous pirate called Redbeard.

"You're going to love it," Dad said to my brother Harry, and me.

Not many people visited the Pirate Museum. Then one afternoon three men arrived. Dad showed them the museum.

"This is Redbeard's telescope and his sword. And these are Redbeard's clothes," Dad said, and he pointed to a model pirate. The three men weren't very interested, but then …

"This is Redbeard's treasure map," said Dad. "Redbeard hid some gold. Nobody knows where it is because we've only got half of the map." The men were *very* interested now.

Suddenly, one of the men shouted, “Now, Dave!”

“OK, Steve,” said Dave, and he pushed Dad. The third man, Phil, grabbed the map.

“What are you doing?” asked Dad. He was angry and afraid.

Steve pulled the other half of Redbeard’s map from his pocket.

“We are looking for Redbeard’s gold,” he said. He put the two pieces of the map together. “And now I know where it is.”

The men were robbers! Steve looked at the map. He didn’t know it but I looked too. The map was of our house!

The robbers pushed us downstairs into the cellar. Phil and Dave started to dig a big hole.

"Look! A tunnel!" said Harry. "It's Redbeard's secret tunnel!"

"Dave, you stay here and watch them," said Steve. "We are going to get the gold." He grabbed my brother. "And this boy is coming with us. The tunnel is small, and so is he!"

The two robbers climbed into the tunnel with Harry.

Dave watched Dad and me. I wanted to run for help, but the robber was between me and the cellar door. Dave was big and very strong, but he wasn't very clever.

"Do you know about Redbeard's ghost?" I asked. "When somebody looks for his gold, the ghost gets angry."

"I don't believe in ghosts," said Dave, but his eyes were big now.

Suddenly, there was a noise behind him.

"What's that?" said Dave.

"It's Redbeard's ghost!" I shouted. Dave jumped back, hit his head and fell to the floor.

Of course, it wasn't Redbeard's ghost. It was our cat!

"What are we going to do? The robbers are going to find the gold!" I said.

Then I had a fantastic idea! I told Dad and he ran upstairs. He told me to wait, but I was worried about Harry.

I climbed into the tunnel. I knew the way because of the map. Suddenly I saw Steve and Phil in a big cave. Then Harry came out of a small cave.

My brother had a big, wooden chest with him. Steve opened the chest and smiled. It was full of gold coins – Redbeard's gold!

"I'm rich!" Steve shouted.

“There’s the girl from the museum!” shouted Phil suddenly.

“Quick! Run!” shouted Harry. But it was too late. Phil grabbed me. He pulled me over to my brother.

“What are we going to do?” Harry asked me in a quiet voice.

“Don’t worry,” I said. “I’ve got a plan. Dad is coming soon.”

The robbers picked up the chest.

But suddenly a man appeared – a pirate! He had a sword and a big, red beard.

"STOP! DO NOT TOUCH MY GOLD!" the pirate shouted.

"Don't worry," I whispered to Harry. "It's Dad wearing Redbeard's clothes from the museum."

But the robbers didn't know this. They were very scared. "Help! It's a ghost!" they shouted. They dropped the chest and ran away.

Suddenly there was another voice behind us.

"I am the ghost of Redbeard!". Dad was standing at another entrance, in pirate clothes.

"Where are the robbers, Megan?" Dad asked.

"They ran away," I said. "You scared them."

"No, I didn't," said Dad. "I've just arrived."

"If you weren't the pirate they saw," I said, "who *was* it?"

Harry's eyes were big. "It was a real ghost, Redbeard's ghost!"

Back at the museum, the police arrested the three robbers.

Dad told the police about the gold.

"The tunnel is under your house," said the police officer. "It's *your* gold."

"That's right," I said. "Redbeard stopped the robbers, but he didn't stop us!"

So now Dad is making the Pirate Museum bigger and better. When we moved here, Dad said to Harry and me, "You're going to love it." He was right!

# Activities

**1 Circle T (True) or F (False).**

1 The World Cup football trophy is gold. (T) F
2 The biggest piece of gold came from South Africa. T F
3 Gold is a very hard metal. T F
4 Goldfinger was a Greek king. T F
5 People usually find gold in rivers. T F
6 Europeans discovered the city of El Dorado. T F
7 In 1848, somebody discovered gold in California. T F
8 Gold is a very cheap metal. T F

**2 Circle the objects that you think have gold in them.**

1

2

3

4
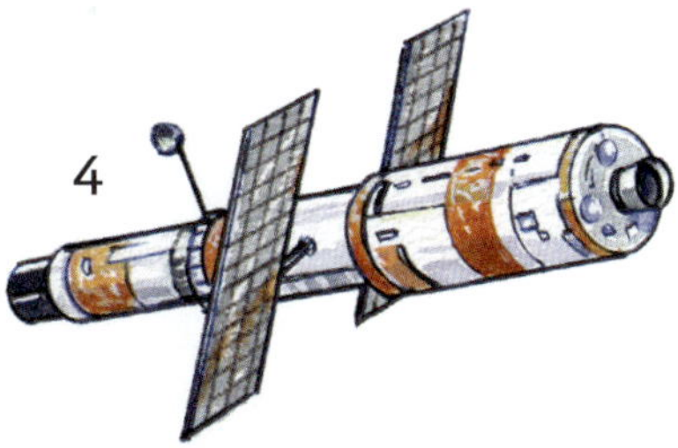
5

6

7

## 3 Read and match.

1 Many of the world's gold mines
2 King Tutankhamun was
3 King Midas turned
4 The Romans used
5 Spanish explorers went
6 Blackbeard was a very
7 The government of the USA keeps its

- to South and Central America.
- gold coins as money.
- are in South Africa.
- a pharaoh in Ancient Egypt.
- gold in Fort Knox.
- his daughter into gold.
- famous pirate.

## 4 Match the sentences in exercise 3 to the pictures by writing a number in each box.

a [4]

b [ ]

c [ ]

d [ ]

e [ ]

f [ ]

g [ ]

**5 Who said what? Match the sentences to the pictures.**

1 This is Redbeard's telescope and his sword.

2 We are looking for Redbeard's gold.

3 STOP! DO NOT TOUCH MY GOLD!

4 It's Redbeard's ghost!

**6 Put the sentences in the correct order.**

The police arrested the robbers. ☐

They saw Redbeard's ghost. ☐

Three men arrived at the Pirate Museum. ☐

Dad opened the Pirate Museum. 1

They took Harry with them into the tunnel. ☐

Steve put the two pieces of the map together. ☐

The robbers dropped the chest and ran away. ☐

## 7 Complete the story with the words in the box.

| arrived | discovered | looked | ~~moved~~ | arrested | |
|---|---|---|---|---|---|
| wanted | opened | saw | stayed | were | grabbed |

Megan's family ___moved___ to a new house. Megan's dad __________ a Pirate Museum. One day three men __________ at the museum. They __________ the treasure map from the museum. They already had the other half of the map. They __________ to find Redbeard's gold. They __________ at the map and __________ a secret tunnel in the cellar. Two of them took Harry into the tunnel. One of the robbers __________ with Megan and her dad. In the tunnel, the robbers discovered the chest. But then they __________ a ghost! They __________ afraid and ran away. The police __________ the robbers.

# Bilingual Dictionary

Write the words in your language.

| | | | |
|---|---|---|---|
| archaeologist | ________ | mask | ________ |
| arrest | ________ | medal | ________ |
| bury | ________ | melt | ________ |
| cave | ________ | mine | ________ |
| cellar | ________ | mobile phone | ________ |
| chariot | ________ | museum | ________ |
| chest | ________ | pirate | ________ |
| coffin | ________ | plan | ________ |
| coin | ________ | real | ________ |
| conquer | ________ | robber | ________ |
| dig | ________ | satellite | ________ |
| electricity | ________ | separate | ________ |
| empire | ________ | shine | ________ |
| entrance | ________ | sink | ________ |
| expensive | ________ | soft | ________ |
| explorer | ________ | statue | ________ |
| find | ________ | steal | ________ |
| ghost | ________ | sweat | ________ |
| government | ________ | sword | ________ |
| helmet | ________ | telescope | ________ |
| history | ________ | touch | ________ |
| hole | ________ | treasure | ________ |
| incredible | ________ | trophy | ________ |
| jewellery | ________ | tunnel | ________ |
| map | ________ | wire | ________ |

Macmillan Education
4 Crinan Street
London N1 9XW
A division of Springer Nature Limited
Companies and representatives throughout the world

ISBN 978-1-3800-3846-3
ISBN 978-1-3800-3774-9 (International Edition)



First published 2007
This edition published 2019



Designed and illustrated by Red Giraffe Limited

The author and publishers would like to thank the following for permission to reproduce their photographs:

Cover photography reproduced with the kind of permission of Corbis/ Peter M. Fisher

Alamy/ PlainPicture GmbH & CO KG p2b, Alamy/ Pictorial press Ltd p10; Alamy Stock Photo/Lebrecht Music & Arts p8, Alamy Stock Photo/Edward Bock p13; Getty Images/Cultura/GP Kidd p14(t), Corbis/ Gideon Mendel p4, Getty Images/ Ian Waldie p2t, Getty/ Erik Simonsen p3, General Photographic Agency p6, Getty/ Robert Harding p7; PhotoDisc/Getty Images p1; Ronald Grant Archive p14b; The Art Archive/ Science Museum London p5, The Art Archive/ Dagli Orti p9t, The Art Archive/ Musée du Louvre, Paris, Dagli Orti p9b.



Printed and bound in Great Britain by Bell and Bain Ltd

2023 2022 2021 2020 2019
10 9 8 7 6 5 4 3 2 1